THE CULTURE BLUEPRINT: BUILDING, IMPLEMENTING, and GROWING THE FOUNDATIONS for ORGANIZATIONAL & TEAM SUCCESS

Published by Chaplain Publishing
Lubbock, Texas
www.chaplainpublishing.com

Copyright © 2020 by Pat Rigsby.

All rights reserved. This work is protected by copyright. No part of this book may be reproduced or transmitted in any form or by any means, including photocopies or scanned images, photographs, or via any other means without express written permission from the publisher.

ISBN: 978-1-941549-50-6

Cover and text design: NiTROhype Creative
www.nitrohype.com

Printed in the United States of America

The CULTURE BLUEPRINT

Building, Implementing, and Growing the Foundations for Organizational & Team Success

CONTENTS

Introduction 6

Leadership 20

Vision 36

Values 46

Standards of Performance 56

Systems 68

People 82

Communication 100

About the Authors 106

THE CULTURE BLUEPRINT

1 *Introduction*

CHAPTER 1: INTRODUCTION

The goal of this book is simple: to help you build a strong culture on your team or in your organization.

It doesn't matter if you're a sport coach building a stronger team, a business owner who wants to create a culture that your staff wants to be a part of, or really any type of organization that you're leading—this blueprint is going to give you the foundation.

It's going to give you the concepts, the tools, and the framework to build a culture that helps you accomplish all of the goals that you set out to put in place as a leader.

WHY SHOULD YOU LISTEN TO ME WHEN IT COMES TO BUILDING CULTURE?

I've got about 20 years of study on this topic. It all started when I became a college baseball coach. I got a head coaching job at the ripe old age of 23 and I took over a program that had never had a winning season.

My first two years we were okay. We were a little bit above .500, so a bit above average, but we just couldn't seem to break through. We couldn't shake that losing culture that had plagued the program to that point.

I really started to dig in and study what building a great culture looked like. I read every book I could find about what great organizations, great teams, and great businesses had in common when it came to establishing and maintaining a strong culture. I starting putting similar principles in place and focused on making it the foundation of our work as a college baseball program.

THE CULTURE BLUEPRINT

The results were great.

We immediately became a nationally competitive program until the time that I was done as a college baseball coach. At the same time, I was a strength and conditioning coach at the university and we had a couple of nationally competitive programs—one that had recently won a national title and one that was a national runner-up. I got to witness what they were doing in developing their culture and even got to play a small part in the successful implementation of their culture, too.

As I moved into building a business, I discovered that many of the same foundational principles applied not just to athletics, but in business pursuits, as well. I worked to establish a successful culture and we grew very rapidly. We had great staff retention. We had great client retention. I started to realize the connection.

Then, as I moved into becoming more of a business coach and working with entrepreneurs around the country and around the globe, I could see that the people who had success in building their own businesses, growing their own teams, retaining clients, and building organizations that people wanted to be a part of all shared a common thread, too.

Over my time as a business owner, I've been fortunate enough to build over 30 different businesses in the fitness and sports performance industry, but a couple of the ones I was most proud of were franchise organizations that not only had success from a monetary sense but were award-winning when it came to franchisee satisfaction. Such is just another way to say "culture."

The parent franchise organization was ranked number one in its category as far as mid-size franchises in North America for three years straight

CHAPTER 1: INTRODUCTION

when it came to franchisee satisfaction. That's not just when it comes to fitness franchises or sports performance franchises, either. That's franchises of any type with under 500 locations throughout North America.

Number one in its category for *three straight years*.

Additionally, the parent company was a multiple-time award winner for "best places to work" in our state. We had great retention of the people who were part of our team. The people who we had coming in to work with us enjoyed working there and wanted to be a part of it. And in my opinion, those accolades are all a manifestation of this same foundation of culture that we are going to talk about in this book.

BUILDING UPON THOSE FOUNDATIONS

Since then, I've continued to read, study, and watch to learn about and from great businesses that have thrived. I've also seen other businesses that lack culture seem to implode. My experiences have taught me to be able to see the things that they were missing and how their lack of positive culture contributed to their demise.

These organizations might have had two or three of the components that we're going to touch on, but they didn't have them akk. As a result, they lacked that strong, solid foundation to build upon and it weakened the very underpinnings of their organization.

As we go through this process together, we will address what it takes to build a great culture. We will address how you can tighten up the areas that you may not yet be strong in. We will work together to build a strong foundation so that you can have the culture

THE CULTURE BLUEPRINT

that attracts the type of people with whom you want to work.

It doesn't matter whether we are talking about players or employees. Together, we will learn how to best attract the people who can support and carry your culture forward. We will learn how to retain them and get them excited to be a part of what you are doing. Your organization's people will become the ambassadors for what you are doing and we will discuss ways to ensure that they are all pulling the proverbial rope in the same direction.

Keep in mind: executing a cultural blueprint is a building-block process. We will break things down step by step until you have the foundation you need to build a powerful championship-level culture that can be used to propel your organization toward further success.

THE CULTURE BLUEPRINT: AN OVERVIEW

First, we want to give you the 40,000-foot view of *The Culture Blueprint*. We will touch on each of the seven components of building a great culture that we have found to be true and—for the most part—universal. However, don't get too caught up in any one of them in particular just yet. We just want you to have a foundational knowledge of each component and how they fit together. That way, when we break them down into separate components, you'll understand how they link together and why they're so important.

Component #1: Leadership

The first step in building a great culture is having great leadership. Without great leadership, nothing else really matters. You can't have a successful culture without great leadership. It's a must. It really sets the

CHAPTER 1: INTRODUCTION

tone for everything else. You, as the person who is reading this book, have to understand and embrace the responsibility that comes with that leadership role. You have to know that you're the one setting the tone for everyone else. You're the one who can be thought of as that first link in the chain that binds everything else together.

If you're not doing a great job as a leader, it's going to be virtually impossible for everyone else to reach their potential and to really feel connected to everything else that is going on the organization. Instead, they're going to feel like a lot of what you claim your organization stands for is without substance. They will probably think that your vision and values are just empty words rather than something supported by true meaning. They're not something that are tangible.

So it starts with you.

In fact, we've all probably seen this at some level. Great coaches take over programs that haven't had a great deal of success, but that change in leadership at the top was the catalyst to trigger a series of changes. There may still have been the same people in place, but the changes elsewhere were tangible. The organization or the team instantly enjoyed more success.

We've also seen the flipside of this: assistant coaches are promoted or new leaders come in and take over. They may even still have all or most of the same people. They may still have been selling the same products or running the same systems or whatever else, but the production, the success, and culture all deteriorate because the leadership was lacking.

Understand that as the leader, those individuals are going to follow—one way or the other. They're going to follow you to success or they're going to follow you to failure. But it starts with you. That's the basis that everything else is built on. Leadership is the first component building a great culture.

Component #2: Vision

The second component is your vision. It is your what and your why. This is a theme or an overarching message that brings everyone together: vision is what you're trying to accomplish and why you're trying to accomplish it.

Whether it's trying to win a national championship and the "why" behind it or the type of business you're trying to build and why that is important, vision defines how your efforts are going to impact the lives of the people that you serve and the people who are involved. At the same time, your vision is the unifying force that you get to serve as the leader to. You are the person who is disseminating the message and it has to be something that you as a leader are truly connected to.

Your company's vision is something that you are going to have to eat and breathe and sleep for it to have true meaning because you're going to have to carry this torch throughout every interaction that you have. You are going to have to be the person who has this permeate throughout everything that you do.

Ultimately, this is a unifying front for everyone else. Done well, the vision serves to inform all involved parties what direction they need to pull. It should serve to influence all aspects of your business as you and your staff consistently recognize and answer opportunities and questions such as "…Wait a minute: this is what we're about. This is why we do what we do. This is what we're trying to accomplish."

CHAPTER 1: INTRODUCTION

The vision is the glue that holds everyone together because they can always reroute. If you think of the vision as the organizational "GPS navigation," all stakeholders can use it to reroute and know that this is where our destination is so we can always get back on track and know where we're trying to go.

Component #3: Values

The third component of building a great culture is your values. We see a lot of people talking about "core values," or more recently, "values-based cultures." Many organizations have used these precepts to trigger transformative change in both what they do and how they are doing it. But simply put, core values could be compared to guardrails: they are the rules by which we're willing to play.

We have to understand that as we are trying to achieve our vision, we are going to use our values to keep us in line so we know how to make decisions on a daily basis. This helps us on our journey as we move toward that vision. However, we must ensure that we are doing it in a way that's congruent with the values of the organization.

Values can serve as the filter that your team members, your employees, your players, or your stakeholders can use as they make decisions.

That's where our values come into play.

Component #4: Standards of performance

The next component of culture building involves standards of performance or our expectations. In many respects, we've somewhat strayed from this concept in a lot of places in society. Most every organization has a vision. Many have values. But with standards of performance, each person has a specific role to play. This added level of accountability can

THE CULTURE BLUEPRINT

be absolutely key in leveling up and ensuring that each person—be they a client in a training business, an athlete on a team, or an employee in any other organization—has a standard of expectation.

Standards of performance have to be clear and specific, serving to define exactly what success should look like. The standard of performance establishes precisely what needs to be met or accomplished if the team or organization is going to achieve the vision.

The standard of performance could be compared to a scoreboard that lets people know whether or not they have effectively played the role they need to play for everyone to achieve the vision of the organization.

Component #5: Systems

Having standards of performance is important; however, without systems, our team members will lack a detailed and specific way to meet them. It seems as though every business guru these days talks about having systems in place. It doesn't matter if you are listening to a high-profile coach or manager talking about the coaching process or a Fortune 500 CEO discussing his or her business best practices—it seems as though this concept is unnecessarily shrouded in mystery for the majority of business owners.

However, the truth of the matter is that a system is nothing more than a repeatable way to meet our standards of performance. It's really just saying, "Hey, this is the job that we have to do. Here's how we can consistently do it so that we meet our standards of performance." It's nothing more than that.

It is not this giant, daunting thing. It doesn't require some huge and ambiguous operations manual that we don't know how to access or use. Instead, it is simply developing a process and defining a consistent

CHAPTER 1: INTRODUCTION

way of doing things that achieve that standard of performance.

Oftentimes, business owners get caught up in the whole idea of operational systems and they assume this component is covered. "Well hey, we've got systems in place," they think. While systems will make you more efficient, if the things that you're more efficient at aren't helping you achieve the vision, then they don't matter. You're becoming efficient at doing nothing useful.

> *While systems will make you more efficient, if the things that you're more efficient at aren't helping you achieve the vision, then they don't matter. You're becoming efficient at doing nothing useful.*

Having systems needs to be the fifth component of the puzzle, but if we don't understand the preceding four and have them in place and fully operational, then our systems don't have much value.

Component #6: People

Next, at number six, we get to people. This includes our teams, players, employees—it is all people-centric. Notice when you see a lot of "experts" talk about culture, they start with people. They'll say things like, "Hey, if you've got great people, that's the core of great culture."

THE CULTURE BLUEPRINT

Well, in some way of looking at this, that's at least partially true. We have to have people. As has been said, "people make the world go 'round." Everything that we do centers around people in our teams and in our businesses.

But consider this: you could have the best people in the world—truly world-class in each of their respective areas. However, if they are not aligned with the vision, then they're not going to reach their potential. It's going to be a job. They're just going to be going through the motions.

Examples from the sports world illustrating this point are plentiful. Consider the New England Patriots and their oft-cited "Patriot Way" culture. Their dominance in the NFL is unparalleled and they have frequently and consistently defeated teams with more high-profile rosters. Meanwhile, their roster tends to consist of athletes who make up for a lack of superstar-caliber physical attributes by a complete buy-in to the Patriot Way system. At the same time, superstars on other teams who might not share similar values might even be great people, but they're not a great fit if they don't line up with the values of their organization. As a result, they and their teams underachieve.

If your team members don't know what the standards of performance are, how can they be expected to succeed? How can they contribute to team victory if you haven't taken the time to help them define what success looks like? If they lack systems to follow, how can you ask them to go out and do great work? You simply must provide your team members with the systems, the foundation, and the framework to meet those standards of performance consistently over time.

So yes, having great people is important. It's

CHAPTER 1: INTRODUCTION

crucial. But incredible talents can still flounder in organizations or as part of teams because the other things weren't in place. Perhaps they lacked a strong leader. Or maybe they didn't have a vision they felt connected with. Regardless, while it is clear that people are the lifeblood of vibrant, growing, and successful organization, without the other components in place, those same people will not be set up to succeed.

Component #7: Communication

Lastly, communication is the glue that holds the entire thing together. Communication serves as the means through which we connect people with all the other components. As a leader, we have to consider a number of critical questions: how are we motivating people? How are we connecting them to the vision? How are we making sure that our values are upheld, that they're regularly part of this, in our team's decision making process? These are essential in ensuring that the messages we send and interpret are appropriate and best suited to reach our aims.

Other questions are important to consider, as well. How are we communicating as an organization top to bottom (not just you as the leader but everyone)? How are we communicating the vision? How are we making sure that everyone embraces the values? How do we make sure that someone knows what is expected of them (the standards of performance)? Or how do we get somebody to understand and really embrace the systems that they need to be successful?

We have to teach. We have to recognize people for what they're doing well. We have to reinforce the behaviors that we want and we have to help people narrow their focus in the event they get off track.

THE CULTURE BLUEPRINT

This is communication—regular, specific, and effective communication.

If we know what we are communicating and we know what the message is, then communication becomes so much easier. Perhaps more importantly, it becomes all that much more powerful.

THE JOURNEY BEGINS

Those are the seven components of building a great culture. If we have these pieces in place, then everything else becomes easier. Probably the best part of this approach is that it's a framework. It's not that you have to lead the exact same way that someone else leads. It's not that yourevision needs to be the same as somebody else's vision or that your values need to match someone else's. It doesn't matter who you admire or anything else. It can be—and most assuredly should be—uniquely your own.

> *If we have those pieces in place, then everything else becomes easier.*

In my case, I learned this lesson early on. I had a coach who I tried to emulate my first couple of years. I quickly discovered that I couldn't lead the way that he led. We were and are different people. We are wired differently and my vision was different than his vision.

Instead, over time, I found my own voice. I learned from him but then I found other people to learn from, too. I used this framework and I applied each of these seven components in a way that rang true to me. And it worked best for my team. And it has

CHAPTER 1: INTRODUCTION

continued to work for my businesses and my coaching clients over the years, too.

That's where we are going and that's where you are headed throughout the remainder of this book. We're going to go through each of these seven components and we are going to help you figure out how this fits into the bigger picture that fits your unique situation. How you choose to fill your box with the things that are true to your goals, your vision, and your style so that you can build, implement, and grow the culture that you want.

WORK IT OUT

Which of the seven components do you think you are strongest within currently? Why?

Which of the seven components do you think you are weakest within currently? Why?

2 Leadership

CHAPTER 2: LEADERSHIP

LEADERSHIP AND THE CULTURE BLUEPRINT

The first thing any leader needs to do upon assuming a new position of authority is to define the way things are done. That's what a culture is, really. It's "the way we do things around here" and "the way we go about our business," and as the leader, you're the one who defines that.

You're the one who sets the tone. As we discussed previously, you're the one who is essentially the first domino to fall in the process. You're the one who is developing other leaders within your organization, so however you lead will set the tone for others. The leaders you train will take on some of your traits.

That doesn't mean that everyone is going to mimic you or model your behavior exactly, but I've seen it so many times in a coaching scenario where a head coach might be like the bad cop and assistant coach is the good cop. Regardless, you're the one still defining, establishing, and to a certain extent enforcing your organization's standards of performance. You reinforce the idea that "this is our vision" and ensure that everyone else picks up on it.

You're going to have to establish this from day one. You define the expected way of doing things as an organization, as a team, and as a business. You set the tone.

THE CULTURE BLUEPRINT

It has been said that for better or for worse, attitude is contagious. It's amazing how a leader who—especially in a small atmosphere (a small team or a small business)—comes in in a bad mood really puts a cloud over everything else. On the other hand, if a leader comes in and he or she is excited, enthusiastic, energetic, and clear about their purpose and their vision then that positivity spreads.

I have worked with fitness pro Todd Durkin for years, and I can go into a gym like his Fitness Quest and immediately feel the difference his attitude has made on the place. Todd has built such a powerful culture and you can just tell everyone who works there feeds off of Todd's energy. In some sense, the people who work there are so bought in to the culture that Todd has worked to create that they have replicated his energy.

They're smiling and they're energetic. They greet people with enthusiasm. There's just this positive energy that permeates throughout the business and that starts with Todd, the leader of the organization. Positive people are attracted to that so they want to work there. It fits them.

At the same time, people who wouldn't be a good fit for that culture are repelled. They wouldn't want to necessarily be a part of such an environment, so they self-select away from it. As the leader, it all starts with you. In fact, you're the one establishing the vision as a whole. You're the one saying (as we will discuss in greater detail in Chapter 3), "Hey, this is what we're trying to accomplish and this is the why behind it."

You're crafting the path that everyone is hopefully going to follow as part of the organization. You're

CHAPTER 2: LEADERSHIP

setting the framework, the boundaries, and the perimeter of what this entire culture is going to be and how you intend for it to flourish and become self-sustaining. In this way, sound leadership can eventually lead to unspoken influence that still serves to provide encouragement and correction simply through the culture.

> *So many ineffective leaders make it about themselves. They make everything focused around their own selfish needs and ambitions instead of the larger mission.*

Another way of thinking about this is that as the leader, you're the caretaker for the mission. So many ineffective leaders make it about themselves. They make everything focused around their own selfish needs and ambitions instead of the larger mission. Sadly, the mission that they're trying to accomplish gets undermined by the agenda they are attempting to push for self-promotion. They become preoccupied with their own personal objectives and glory or by enjoying the spotlight for themselves.

Instead, as a committed leader, you're the caretaker of this mission. It's your job to make sure things get done. It's your job to make sure everyone else reaches their potential and meets their standards of performance. It's your job to hire the right people and to groom them and to train them to be successful.

Ultimately, it's your job to coach.

THE CULTURE BLUEPRINT

That's really what leadership is all about. In many cases, it's a blend of being the caretaker of the overarching vision or mission and coaching people up to be best prepared to enact it. It is developing everyone else to lead and to reach their own potential. Ultimately, as a leader, it all comes back to you.

Everything comes back to you.

In fact, I like to tell the entrepreneurs with whom I work, "It's your fault, all the time. Everything is your responsibility." Some people don't like that. They don't want that responsibility and that's okay. If that's truly the case, then you probably shouldn't be in a leadership position. But if you do (and I suspect you do, because that's why you're reading this book) you embrace that.

You want that responsibility because you know that you're capable of making a difference. You know that you're capable of having a profound impact. You know that if you're going to bring someone onto your team—the "people" part of this blueprint—it's your responsibility to bring the right people on. As a leader, it's your duty to make sure that they're aligned with your vision and that your vision can motivate them so that it is more than a job. For the coach, if it's a player, then you believe that they are someone who fits with where you're trying to go as a program.

You're creating systems to set them up to succeed. You're establishing standards of performance so that they know what success looks like. They know what they have to do for the organization to get to where we are trying to go and the role they're going to have to play for us to achieve our overall vision. Simply put, you must ensure that their values line up with your values—and ultimately, they become our values.

This is your responsibility as a leader.

CHAPTER 2: LEADERSHIP

This is your job to make sure that this person comes on and not only fits, but they're set up to succeed. And it all comes back to you. If something goes undone, it's on you. You either got the wrong person to do it or you didn't prepare them to do it well. If we didn't meet our goals, ultimately it comes back to you as a leader. As a result, so much of this is about personal responsibility and accepting that as the cost of aspiring to lead greatly.

I suspect that that's not a problem for you, but it's something that sometimes we lose sight of. We see things in a "micro" sense and we say, "Well this person didn't hold up their end of the bargain. They didn't do their job." But ultimately, did we get the right person to do the job? Did we empower them to do the job well? It all comes back to us. As a leader, that's where we fit into this whole culture blueprint. Building a complete, powerful, successful culture requires you to set the tone for everything else. That's the role leadership plays in this bigger picture.

BECOMING A BETTER LEADER

How you can be more effective, more successful, and develop and use the tools you need to maximize your role as a leader? To follow are a number of proven strategies to become a better leader. But before we dig in, I need to clarify that I didn't invent these things. I've studied many great leaders and leadership experts from people like John Maxwell and Patrick Lencioni, to great coaches, and great CEOs, and I've drawn things and assimilated them into my own businesses and developed my own philosophy. What I want to do is give you a framework within which you're going to fill in what is most appropriate for you as it relates to these five categories.

THE CULTURE BLUEPRINT

Principle #1: As a leader you have to provide a compelling vision of the future

You have to be able to provide a vision that really motivates your people and attracts the right people. As was popularized in Jim Collins' classic business book *Good to Great*, it begins with "getting the right people on the bus." If you have that compelling vision, more people are going to want to be part of what you're doing, and they're going to see this as a career, as a mission, as a passion, and not just as a job. What you are trying to build is a n organization that doesn't just offer being part of a team but rather something bigger. They're trying to move something forward at a greater level.

You have to be able to not only establish that vision, but you have to be able to convey it. There are so many different ways to convey your vision as a leader and this is deeply rooted in personality. Some people can get in front of a group and just light up the room. They have that "Tony Robbins persona" where they're just high-energy with a big personality.

Others are more subdued. They convey this vision in a one-on-one fashion. Personally, through my leadership journey, I've gravitated more toward the one-on-one. Regardless of which comes more naturally to you, being in front of a room is something that we all have to do in that leadership role. You have to find a style that fits for you.

It is critical to understand that the bigger goal, the bigger the accomplishment it is in establishing this vision that gets you where you're trying to go. It can also serve to inspire the people with whom you are working. You have to ask yourself how you convey this to your team and how you compel them to buy in.

CHAPTER 2: LEADERSHIP

Principle #2: Motivate people to perform

It's one thing to establish a vision, rally the troops, and say, "Hey, this is what we're going to do." It's another to see that initial motivation through to thorough, complete, and effective execution. Back in the days when I was coaching college baseball, this vision started with an idea of building a championship program where we were going to go play at the World Series-level. We started with the usual approach in athletics: get great catch phrases printed on t-shirts, paint the logo on the side of the clubhouse, and generally talk things up.

However, there's an entirely different side of this that is really the more important piece: how do you get someone to punch the clock and do the work on a daily basis? How do you inspire a team member to move step by step, incrementally toward this vision? How do you get someone to execute on this mission day after day and understand that they are building toward something bigger?

To reach our fullest potential as an organization, we need each member of the team pursuing excellence on their own. Once that starts to occur, then we can begin to pursue the synergies that spring from it where the sum (the organization or team) is

> ***To reach our fullest potential as an organization, we need each member of the team pursuing excellence on their own.***

27

THE CULTURE BLUEPRINT

even more effective than the components that make it up (individual team members, coaches, and other support staff). For this to really work, stakeholders can't just be doing the job or going through the motions. They can't just show up and give half-hearted effort. They have to be purposefully working towards this vision. And it has to be everyone.

A highly successful baseball coach with whom my (TB) students have worked was an assistant at a number of major programs before he finally got his current position at a Power 5 school. Over the years, he grew to believe deeply in this notion that team success is a result of the efforts of everyone involved with the program. Since taking over as head coach nearly a decade ago, the results have been remarkable. He has taken our team to the NCAA Division I College World Series four times in eight years. He's captured three conference championships, was named National Coach of the Year twice, and our program has had 48 MLB draft picks come from the roster he and his staff built. That kind of success is no accident.

Our academic program once had to reassign a student to another clinical assignment away from the baseball team because, despite being given several opportunities to do so, the student had not convinced this coach that he was "all in." The student would show up late, appear disinterested or disengaged at times, or generally just not seem to care about being excellent in all things. The coach's philosophy was that the team was aspiring to do great things and compete for a national championship, and if one person in the clubhouse didn't share in that vision and pursue it themselves, it would ultimately trickle down and pollute the collective team attitude toward great aspirations. In an unprecedented move, we

CHAPTER 2: LEADERSHIP

had to reassign the student because his actions were interfering with the culture the coach had worked so hard to create.

Again, there are so many ways to approach this and as we move forward through these other steps, we'll be able to break down some of these further. We will better understand how you're going to get someone to dive into standards of performance, understand what their role is, and how that role connects with that bigger vision. But, ultimately, it comes back to you. As their leader, it's your job to make sure people are executing on it—and if not, help them to find a seat on another bus.

Principle #3: You have to lead by example, because people buy people

You can say, "We're going to treat this organization like a family. We're going to treat our clients like family. We're going to have a relationship-centric business. Instead of just thinking ourselves as a team, we're a family." Saying it is easy. Actually doing it though? That's harder.

If you are not authentic and not someone who really leads by example, not only will people be skeptical of you, but they're going to be skeptical of the vision as a whole. They are likely to be left feeling like the entire organization is built on a foundation of sand.

How often do you see a successful sports team where the leader is often talking about a bigger vision and how the organization has been put together, and then the next thing you know, we find out that this person isn't exactly who they made themselves out to be? There's going to be skepticism moving forward. If they do have the opportunity to get another job, there's

THE CULTURE BLUEPRINT

going to be skepticism from the players, the staff, the administration, and in the case of high school and college sports, from the parents of the recruits.

It isn't exclusive to sports, though. We see this over and over in business. I see plenty of people talking about their core values and they like to sing them from the rooftops.

But, they don't live them.

They talk about being a great place to work, but they don't have great employee retention. There's a disconnect there. They don't have people that really feel like they get to have that role in the business. Instead, they get to have a job.

Understand that as we talked about before, it all starts with you. You are the first domino before everything else. You have to be a good role model. But how do you do this? It starts with just being authentic. It starts with telling the truth, and just putting who you are out there and wearing your personal identity on your sleeve. You don't have to try to be someone that you're not.

I know for me, one of the things that I recognized in my first couple of years as a coach was that I wasn't necessarily secure in myself. I got a head coaching job at a university at the ripe old age of 23 and I was so close in age to the student athletes that I felt like I had to be somebody that I wasn't. I had to be this really demanding drill sergeant and really force people to toe the line, even more than I ever would have as a coach. I tried to adopt the philosophies, and the persona of these more rigid, more demanding, more drill sergeant-style coaches, and it didn't fit me. And I know that it caused a disconnect.

People didn't necessarily buy into the vision as much. They didn't necessarily buy into me as much,

CHAPTER 2: LEADERSHIP

either, because I wasn't being authentic. I wasn't leading by example, because they could tell that I behaved one way in a non-work setting, but entirely differently in the clubhouse or on the field.

Principle #4: You have to manage people's performance effectively and hold them accountable

You are responsible for setting standards of performance and asking people to meet them. However, you've got to be consistent. It's not enough to just put it out there and say, "Hey, this is what being successful in your role looks like," and then provide little to no additional guidance (or worse, to get upset when they fail to meet your poorly-specified expectations).

We have to be able to set a standard of performance and hold people accountable to that so that they know whether they are meeting the bar, exceeding the bar, or otherwise failing to even meet the bar of your expectations.

My experience is that virtually everybody wants to be great at what they do. Sure, there are exceptions. There are some people who are just indifferent, but that's the exception, not the rule. Most people want to feel like they did a good job at whatever they did today. They get some personal validation from that.

However, we need to be able to manage that performance and specifically define what a "good job" looks like. We need to have a black and white framework for them to understand what success is in their role. That's standard of performance.

If we don't, then we're not going to be able to manage them effectively. Sure, we can give them a "rah-rah" speech and motivate them for the day, but what are we really motivating them to accomplish? To be busy? To be active? To work harder? That's great, but work harder in what context?

Is it working harder at something that's going to move us toward achieving that overall vision? A key task as a leader it to help others manage their own performance and hold them accountable.

Principle #5: *You need to provide an environment that gives the people who are on the team the support and the opportunity they need to develop*

Again, as the leader, this one is on you. You have to be able to say, "We're going to support you as a member of this team. We're going to support you as a person. And, you know what? We believe in you. You belong to something bigger, and we know what you're capable of becoming."

Some of this is just that intangible side of providing support. Just letting people know that you're on their side, that you believe in them, and you know that they can do great work can be of particular benefit. But that's not enough. You also have to empower them to do that great work. You have to provide the opportunity to develop them so that they can reach their potential within the confines of what you're trying to do.

As we alluded to previously, as you go through these various components of building championship culture, we're going to address this in more detail when we talk about building systems. That's part of the development process. It is giving a team member the systems they need to successfully and consistently execute the tasks we ask of them.

We're going to dig deeper into that, but

CHAPTER 2: LEADERSHIP

understand that it is your job to provide the framework so that someone can feel like when they are ready to develop in their role that they will be supported, that people will believe in them, and they are not out on an island.

Ultimately, when I think of this as a coach, as a leader, as an owner, or as a manager (or whatever leadership role you're in), I think of a number of basic underlying themes. Am I being someone who I would want to work or play for? Am I being someone who I would buy into? Am I creating a vision that will excite people and really be a representation of what I think is possible and where I want to go? Am I getting people to buy into that on a daily basis and see that bigger picture and understand how the things that they're doing today relate to this bigger vision? Am I just being a good person? Am I leading by example or am I basically talking the talk but not walking the walk?

Ultimately, I need to know if I am managing people so that they know when they're being successful versus when they are falling a little bit short. I'm giving them the recognition that they deserve when I catch them doing something right—winning and succeeding. I'm reinforcing the positives and I'm recalibrating on the things that perhaps don't go so well. Am I doing that in a way that if I were on the other side of the desk or if I were one of the players in the field, would I want to play for me?

> *If I were on the other side of the desk or if I were one of the players in the field, would I want to play for me?*

THE CULTURE BLUEPRINT

Would I be the type of leader that I'd say, "Yeah, you know what? That's somebody that I can get on the bus with."

PUTTING IT INTO ACTION

That's the way that I look at this. Those are five general principles and how you're going to execute on those will determine to a large extent just how effective you can be. But it's more than just checking the boxes for you, too. As the leader, there's a personality aspect that you have to figure out, too. What's your preferred leadership style and how are you usually most effective in connecting with those working under your leadership?

Everything can be modified and adapted to best suit your needs, but you have to be consistent and effective in addressing all five principles if you're going to be a successful leader.

CHAPTER 2: LEADERSHIP

WORK IT OUT

What are the key attributes or character qualities you'd use to describe your leadership style?

Which of the five leadership principles resonates with you the most? Why?

3 *Vision*

CHAPTER 3: VISION

THE VISION AND MISSION OF YOUR ORGANIZATION

One of the things that we get into trouble with when it comes to creating a culture is making things unnecessarily complex by adding too many layers and/or too many components. I want to simplify this and I want you to just think about what your vision is, because our vision is really an encapsulation of what we are today and where we want to be. It's who we are and what we do.

When we think about our organization, it starts with leadership. But what about the leader's vision? Where is the organization and where does it need to go? Everything that we're going to do moving forward should really be designed to uphold where we are and maintain that and build on it in order to accomplish the vision.

You may already be outstanding at what you do. You may be the leader in your field—it doesn't matter if we're talking about a sports organization or a truly successful business—but if you are at or near the top, you have to maintain that status. You have to continue to assert yourself as being world-class or first place in your category.

But we always want to improve. We always have that aspiration to be better. When I think about our vision, it's really our leadership articulating what we aspire to be known for as a business. It should also

THE CULTURE BLUEPRINT

serve as the proverbial carrot dangling in front of us, driving and fueling that progress. The vision should motivate us to continue to improve and further inspire innovation. We have to continue to move forward, and that vision is that unifying front.

We've all heard the trite sayings like, "If you're staying the same you're actually losing ground." There's wisdom in such sentiments. We have to continue to move forward and that vision is that unifying front. If we don't have people on our team aligned with the vision who are willing to pursue it within the guard rails of our values are, then they're just trading time for money. They're just there for a job. They don't view their role as a career that they're passionate about.

On the other hand, if they really connect with who we are, what we do, and where we aspire to go, now they have purpose in what they're doing. They're not just watching the clock. They're not just showing up to get done. They're trying to get better, they're trying to make a difference, and they're trying to make an impact. And that's so much of what this component in building a great culture is about.

When we think about our vision, it's this unified front where we're all in this pulling in the same direction. We're trying to do something together. We're trying to accomplish something that, in truth, we probably couldn't accomplish individually. As a result, we have to be crystal clear about what that vision is.

I've seen it so many times. When someone lacks clarity on what they're really trying to accomplish, they just go through the motions (at best). It reminds me of the movie Office Space, where I have to fill out my TPS reports and I have to make sure the covers are

CHAPTER 3: VISION

right. In mind-numbing repetition, work gets done but goals are never achieved. In such situations, no one is considering the big picture goal. Questions like "Who are we?" and "What are we trying to accomplish?" are never asked, let alone answered. You're not going to inspire people in a cubicle with vague, purposeless direction like, "Hey, here's the work you have to get done this week." Just. No.

Instead, consider questions like "Why are we doing this?" "Why is this important?" "What kind of impact is it going to make?" When we think about our vision, that's really where it fits into this larger puzzle. Our vision is us articulating the current state of the business and where we aspire to go.

Hopefully, you're seeing this start to come together. You're seeing that leadership is the lynchpin that holds everything together. With poor leadership, nothing else really matters. At the same time, our vision helps us articulate the current state of the business and where we aspire to go. Our overriding goal is to craft our vision to fit what we want our culture to be and what we want the success of our organization to look like.

DEVELOPING YOUR VISION

If vision is the destination, strategy is the road we take to get there. Building and developing your vision is critical because your vision is like a snapshot of what your future organization will look like. For me, vision gives you focus, motivation, and direction. It gives you clarity so that you know when you're making your strategic plan, you're still moving toward that vision. That's really where you're trying to go.

Different people approach developing their vision in different ways. Some just like to have this simple,

THE CULTURE BLUEPRINT

short, pithy thing. Others want something that's really quantitative. Still others prefer something that's more qualitative.

Again, this is very much up to you. You may say, "We want to play at a championship level. We want to graduate players, and we want to develop good people." You may say, "We want to be the preeminent sports performance program or sports performance organization in our market." It doesn't really matter if it accomplishes those things, if your vision gives you that motivation, focus, and direction, then it is serving a valuable purpose.

Consider these three examples of the way that organizations approach clarifying their vision. I think this would be pretty illustrative of how widely things can range. For Disney—a company that I really pay a lot of attention to—it is pre-eminently service-centric. I naturally gravitate toward this model because so much of what I do professionally falls into this category.

Their vision is simply to make people happy. We think about that, but it's this beacon. Everything they do—whether in major motion pictures, theme parks, toys, or any other commercial pursuit—it all centers around making people happy. "Is this movie going to make our audience happy?" "Is this new attraction or this new land, or even a new park going to make our customers, our guests, happy?" Such guides everything the Walt Disney Company does.

For them, service and making the customer happy is guiding beacon to help in any decision-making process. It's not necessarily a quantitative thing like, "Hey, we want to be a million (or billion)-dollar company." Instead, it is more focused around a theme that serves as a foundation for literally everything else

CHAPTER 3: VISION

they do.

We can compare that to Nike, who says, "Okay, we want to bring innovation and inspiration to every athlete in the world. Basically, if you have a body, you're an athlete." They've got this as their vision. They seek to impact every person in the world through inspiration and innovation.

Now that's big.

I don't necessarily know that they're capable of impacting every person, but that's their driver. That vision is the engine that powers them and the fuel that motivates them. That singular idea provides focus, motivation, and direction. This is what they make sure their people are executing towards.

If we compare that to Apple, their vision is to produce high-quality, low cost, easy-to-use products that incorporate technology for the individual (I think the argument can be made that it's not necessarily low cost, comparatively speaking, but again, that's their guiding light). They're very focused on serving individuals. They have crafted their company to be highly focused on individual consumers and not necessarily driven by selling to corporations. At the same time, they have also focused on high-quality, leading-edge, and disruptive technologies.

You can make the way that you clarify your vision more specific, For example, a college baseball team's vision might include something along the lines of "Hey, we want to play in a world series," or, "We want to be an annual playoff program." Likewise, a small business may aspire to "...impact 10,000 people in their local community in the next 10 years."

The vision can be anything that really helps narrow the focus or help move you faster and further. Obviously, we're not trying to break this down into

THE CULTURE BLUEPRINT

all these incremental components. That's not what your vision is designed for. Instead, when we get into that strategic plan, it is important to develop practical strategies or marching orders to help execute the vision. That's when we want to get even more specific in sorting out the details. If it helps you set your direction, identify your priorities, and helps people grow together or challenges them to improve and become better, then we've done our job in establishing the vision.

FURTHER DEFINING YOUR VISION

Let me give you a few tips in developing the vision for your organization. First, you need to think about where you want your organization to be three to five years from now. A lot of people will tell you five, or 10, or 20 years, but I think that we all can accept at this point that things are changing faster now than they ever have in the past.

Technology has accelerated the rate of change, growth, or evolution in almost every field. I think that if I try to look back 10 years in the past, or 20 years in the past, my vision would be so off-track compared to where I am. So my advice is to forecast and aim for five years of less.

I think to have an effective vision, that it has to be something that's attainable. It may be challenging. It may really be something that you're using to bring out the best in you and really motivate you to go further and faster than you thought possible. But it has to be attainable.

When someone talks about their 20-year vision, I look back 20 years ago, and I was in year three as a college baseball coach. I've been through a variety of iterations of a career since then. It's just so hard to

CHAPTER 3: VISION

predict the future that far out. That gives you enough runway to make some impact, to make some changes, to drive initiatives forward, and really do what you want to do but at the same time it is short enough to be clear. It's not hazy, it's not foggy, and you can actually see that.

Then, three to five years out you recalibrate, readdress, and update the vision with the understanding that your organization has made some progress toward the goals, and can now either continue or adjust toward new targets. In some cases, you may set a vision three years out only to find that you've accomplished it in 18 months. In that case, it is far better to have a vision that accommodate this rate and allow you to readjust and keep growing. You may say, "Okay, we're here. It's time to move forward again."

Secondly, we need to make sure that our vision lines up with our values. I see people all the time who come up with a vision that doesn't line up with who they really are. In the business world, people will say, "Well hey, I want to build a business that impacts 500 clients and has some massive amount of revenue," and all these other things. But when you look, some of their values are about balance and family and if you really dig deep, it would appear that they don't want to work that much.

It might mean that they're trying to grow by 500% over a certain timeframe. But they're also trying to cut their workload simultaneously. You have to make sure that your values, your guardrails, and what you're trying to accomplish are factored in to whatever the vision is that you're trying to establish. The vision has to give you focus and clarity.

I would encourage you to be more specific,

because in a lot of instances, that's going to help you keep people on track. If you give someone really ambiguous, vague guidelines and you make it less clear than it needs to be, you're giving them a lot of margin to interpret it however they want. Doing so will make it harder for people to get excited about their role and their tasks. Instead, it is better to strive for clarity and conciseness.

The vision has to be easy for people to understand, because we all gravitate toward things that we understand. A confused mind says, "No." We need people to really connect with what we're doing and if they can wrap their head around it then it can provide motivation and excitement. If your stakeholders can move toward this, then we've got something special that we can build an entire organization around.

LEVERAGING YOUR VISION

In truth, there's no right or wrong way to develop your vision for your organization. The key is that it has to resonate with you. And perhaps at least as importantly, it has to resonate with your people so that it excites you. It's a reflection of where you actually want to go.

This is not just some arbitrary thing that you haphazardly pull from somewhere else. It needs to be generated from within and it needs to connect with every aspect of your unique situation. It has to inspire you. It has to excite you to get up and go to work every day. And it has to give you direction so that when you're making decisions, it can all be tied back to the vision.

If you say that your vision is to accomplish a certain thing or to reach a certain level, then your vision serves the purpose of providing a reference or

CHAPTER 3: VISION

a standard of comparison. Each decision should be considered by asking, "If I take this path, is it going to lead me toward my vision, or will it pull me off course?" This helps take some of the emotion out and allows the leader to focus on the straightforward reality. You shouldn't overcomplicate this. Instead, just think about where you want to be three to five years from now, articulate that in a simple, clear way, and you've got a pretty good start on having a vision that you can build around.

WORK IT OUT

Write your personal vision statement here:

Write your organizational vision statement here:

THE CULTURE BLUEPRINT

4 Values

CHAPTER 4: VALUES

THE ROLE OF VALUES

When you consider this whole building block process, you begin to see how all the components we've discussed so far stack together. We start with leadership, move on to vision, then specify our values. Values are frequently referred to as "core values" if that's the terminology you'd prefer to use, as such terminology points out how central values need to be to the leadership and the vision. What I've witnessed in great teams, great businesses, and in world-class organizations is how these values serve as a filter for decision making.

Values-based decision making is a process where every choice is run through a series of values-related questions. "Is this us? Does this fit what we do, who we are, what we're about?" Or, alternatively, is an opportunity maybe not a great fit and therefore something you should avoid? It doesn't necessarily matter if it is going to add to the bottom line or if it is going to get you more victories on the field. If it isn't aligned with your purpose, then simply put, it's a distraction.

> *If it isn't aligned with your purpose, then, it's a distraction.*

THE CULTURE BLUEPRINT

But how do we derive these values and where should they come from? Without specified values, many people lack these decision making filters and instead are left to make decisions emotionally. Choices are made absent the ability to strategically consider the larger picture about building what you are trying to accomplish through that vision that we've talked about. Such is a missed opportunity, as these are connecting points for your team's beliefs. They're things that your team identifies with and they can serve as unifying threads that run through the entire organization.

For example, if someone comes into the organization and they fail to connect with the values, then they most likely will not be able to make good decisions on behalf of the organization day after day. This doesn't mean that their personal values have to line up perfectly with your organizational values. But people do have to connect with them. They have to believe in them. They have to be willing to say, "Look, I'm willing to be an ambassador for this."

And if they do, now they can go out and make good decisions because that's so much of what our people do: they make choices that ultimately are representations of our greater organization.

CONNECTING THROUGH VALUES

Most fundamentally, values are the best qualities of our organization distilled down to what we believe about ourselves. Put another way, they are the way that we want to make choices so that ultimately we do accomplish our vision. And they Are usually deeply held beliefs about our organization.

Values are those beliefs that we feel that—if we are able to uphold them—we're going to consistently

CHAPTER 4: VALUES

make good decisions and represent ourselves in a way that we want to be represented time and time again.

And they're that beacon, if you will, or that guiding light that allows you to reign yourself back in whenever you are faced with choices. Whenever you are faced with different paths that we can follow, these are the guardrails that you use to make sure you stay on track to where you're trying to go.

Plus, it's a great way for you to essentially say, "Look, we're on track for our long-term objective, not necessarily short-term gratification, but the values that we hold is the foundation. It is the core of what we do."

Values are not just some sign on a wall or something on the "About Us" on our website or in a locker room. These are the things that you know that if you are trying to describe your organization and what it stands for, you can distill it down in a few sentences or bullet points to say, "This is what we're about."

When thinking about those seven steps to building a great culture, a lot of times people think about their goal but they don't think about the way they make decisions to get there. For example, you think about those standards of performance that your people have to meet, but you don't think about the guardrails people have to stay within in order to meet them.

Obviously, we'll talk about how to develop your values and how to best articulate them so that they can become the foundation of what you do, but it is important to give you an overview of how this fits in to this entire seven-step process to build the culture that you want.

DEVELOPING YOUR VALUES

Values should be specific, but they should also

THE CULTURE BLUEPRINT

still be "big picture." Developing your values is a process, but they should really just be a reflection of who you already are. What's great about values is that they help guide your decision-making process and will serve as guardrails as you move toward the destination that you're trying to achieve.

Examples of values might include something like the following: "Our organization is built on honesty and integrity." "We're growth-oriented." "We're committed." "We're teamwork-focused." "We're an organization that prizes accountability." "We're an organization that really is focused on an attention to detail."

You can come up with any or all of the well-crafted sayings you want, but what's particularly powerful about establishing your values is that they serve to set the tone for your organization. Not only that, values also help you better define who you are personally, what you're all about, and how you go about making your decisions.

Another benefit of developing your values is that they serve not only to attract the right people, they also serve to repel the wrong people who are not a good fit for your organization. When your values resonate with potential employees, team members, or partners, it is likely to trigger them into action toward you and your organization. Those people say or think, "Hey, this is somewhere that I belong." Likewise, those who don't align with your values tend to move in a different direction.

For example, when I (TB) was looking for a position as an athletic trainer working with Division I football, I was most interested in finding a spot at a private faith-based institution. I felt that that setting would offer me not just the professional growth I

CHAPTER 4: VALUES

was looking for, but also the personal and spiritual fulfillment I wanted. I gravitated toward a particular school that was well known for its adherence to its faith-based mission and ultimately got a position there. However, I had friends in the profession who made it clear that they would never even consider working at my school due to the University's outspoken views and professed values. Anyone who had an issue with the values of my school would have had a challenging time working there, so publishing those values was of benefit to all.

Your values help you make decisions on how you recognize or how you reward. They can also serve as highly specific tools to help you review the success (or lack thereof) of someone who is a part of your organization. And most importantly, they are a powerful mechanism to help you know what is a good decision or who is a good fit for your organization.

That's all fine and good, and by now you probably get all that. But the question you're probably asking is "How do we establish our values? How do we pick the right values for our organization?" And whether you realize it or not, they're actually already there. For better or worse, they're already in place. While they may or may not be written down, they are woven into everything that already goes on. There's an assumption that people "kind of know" what your values are—or more specifically, the types of knowledge, skills, and abilities as well as the overall experiences and expectations that you have. But maybe there's never been a true focal point to guarantee that everyone understands and can build upon them.

As we get into four questions that should help you extract the values from your business, we just have to accept that whatever emerges will likely exist only to help you stay true to who you are. If you want to change the culture, you'll have to be purposeful about specifically addressing the values, as they will continue to serve as those proverbial guardrails that define what you want to be known for.

#1: *What image do you want to convey?*

What do you want to be known for? It doesn't matter if we're talking about to the marketplace, to prospective recruits, or to prospective employees—what do you want people to know about you? Because if this is who you are, you can't assume that people know on the outside what goes on inside your four walls. You want to make sure that you're conveying the things that you feel are important because it's a great vetting process. It helps people know if you're a good fit. Consider the message and think more in terms of what goes on within your organization that you feel is important enough for people outside to know about.

#2: *What are your organization's underlying philosophies?*

This one is very much related to the first question, however, I'm sure that you and/or your organization have some things that serve as drivers regarding how you go about your business. For me, my underlying philosophy that guides many of my business decisions even today is that I want to do fewer things better. I want simple because I think that common sense isn't always common practice. Those types of things are underlying philosophies for me. I want to be relationship-driven and for my organization and my business, those underlying philosophies are things that I want to weave into my values.

CHAPTER 4: VALUES

Consider the philosophies within your organization that drive the way that you do business. Maybe you've never documented them in a written way before or framed them as values, but you know what philosophies have helped you get to where you are. As a result, if you focus on them and you clarify them, they can and most likely will drive you even further forward.

> *Common sense isn't always common practice.*

#3: What are your personal values?

This is something I think often gets lost in the role of being a leader. The world doesn't work in a way that allows us to just have this clear division where we are able to say, "Okay. Personal is *here* and professional is *there*." It just doesn't.

I'm sure that you've seen it and I've seen it, as well. In fact, most business books that I've encountered suggest that it should be precisely that way. However, if you're going to be true to yourself and authentic in your leadership style, you need to make sure that your organization's values are in line with your own personal values.

What are your personal values? For me, it's family first. When I make decisions professionally, I'm often making that decision. In fact, if family first is one of my values (and it is), one of the ways that I make my decisions is that I don't go away for more than two consecutive nights for work unless a member of my family comes with me.

Does that limit some of the things that I could do professionally, to grow my business? Sure.

THE CULTURE BLUEPRINT

But it also forces me to say, "How can I grow my business while not taking those extra trips and staying those extra days?" Think about what your personal values are and how they would permeate through the way that you currently do business and the way you want to do business as you grow and expand. In this way, your personal values aren't something to be hidden or overcome but rather a strength to be leveraged.

#4: *What are your team's values?*

Think about your best people—the people who are the embodiment of what you want your team to be now and in the future. What are the values that they share? This is a valuable exercise because if we are able to recognize this common thread that runs through ourselves and the people who we feel are the right folks to have on our bus, then they should probably be reflected in our organization's values so that we're attracting more of those types of people. This serves to provide more congruency within our organization where really the culture is stronger because people are like-minded and they share similar values.

Look at the people that you have and think about what makes them special or unique. I'm not saying that you just adopt their values verbatim, but if you can blend what you see as the philosophical drivers to your success in the business along with what the team and your best people share, then you have a recipe for success. If we see all this coming together, then it should be reflected in our organization's values as a whole.

CHAPTER 4: VALUES

DRIVING IT HOME

Values are a critical piece to implementing a culture of success because they serve as valuable reference points against which decisions may be compared. Over time, the hope is that the values of the organization not only serve to better define and establish who the organization is and what it stands for, but also attracts like-minded talent that can help further develop that reputation. Furthermore, by integrating the values of the individual team members with that of the organization, stakeholders are likely to take greater ownership in the team, potentially propelling all further, faster, and better toward the intended target or outcome.

WORK IT OUT

Write your top 3-5 most important personal value statements here:

Would you say that your organization's values align with your own? Why or why not?

# 5

Standards of Performance

CHAPTER 5: STANDARDS OF PERFORMANCE

WHAT IS EXPECTED OF OUR TEAM MEMBERS IN ORDER TO ACCOMPLISH THEIR ROLE IN ACHIEVING OUR VISION?

The next component of building a complete and successful culture are the standards of performance that you have for each person who comprises your organization. This is an opportunity that I think so many organizations miss on. If you aren't clear about what's expected, then clarity suffers and accountability is undermined.

It doesn't matter if we're hiring someone to be a part of our staff and we just "throw them in" or if it's a longstanding member of our team; if they don't know what they have to do in order to be successful, then it is difficult for them to hold up their end of the bargain. How can you meet standards of performance when no one has taken the time to even define them for you? It is a recipe for failure.

When we think about a person who we bring in, the first thing we have to think about is whether they have the aptitude to meet our standards of performance. Can they accomplish what we need to accomplish in this role to achieve our vision and basically play their part in the greater cause of achieving that vision or not? Sometimes we put people in the wrong seat. And when they inevitably fail—and they oftentimes will—it is in no small part because we set them up to fail.

THE CULTURE BLUEPRINT

We don't give them an opportunity to succeed because maybe they don't have the skillset to meet those standards of performance. It is something that I see happen time and time again. But then we can also think about whether or not they even know what success looks like. Does the person in a particular role know what would constitute success? Because so often they don't. Things are ambiguous.

As well-renowned researcher and speaker Brené Brown has said, unclear is unkind. Clear is kind. If we want our team members to grow and to be held accountable for that growth, we owe them clarity. But so often, we are unclear. And at its core, that lack of clarity is unkind.

I see it frequently in the personal training community: a trainer gets hired to go and train clients. The expectation is fairly clear that this person will come in and deliver training sessions. However, everything else is really ambiguous. But then I'll hear the business owner say, "Well, this person isn't driving business. They're not selling. They're not bringing anything in."

However, to everyone but that disgruntled or disappointed owner, that wasn't part of the standards that were passed onto the new hire. They were never told that that was part of the expectation. If we want to set someone up for success, we start with a job description. We need to start with very specific expectations of what our stakeholder is expected to do to succeed in this job. If we are clear, then we communicate that these are the standards you have to meet if our organization is going to be successful.

With those expectations clearly established, then we have to make sure that our people have the aptitude and the willingness to do it and they can do

CHAPTER 5: STANDARDS OF PERFORMANCE

it within our values and stay within the guardrails that we have established through our values. Basically, we're giving them the proven processes to make sure that they can meet these standards of performance consistently (more on that in Chapter 6).

However, if we haven't told anyone what the standards are and we haven't reinforced them continually, then how can we expect them to succeed? How can we expect them to know what—at least so far—exists only in our head?

WHAT DOES SUCCESS LOOK LIKE?

How often have you seen or heard someone in management, leadership, or ownership who is disgruntled with the performance of a team member but at the same time that team member doesn't even know what's expected of them, in a really clear, and specific way? As has been covered previously, our leadership sets the tone for everything. But within that, you've got your vision that defines what you're aspiring to be, who you are, and what you want to be known for. You also have your values to guide your operations.

But now you've got your standards of performance. This is when you get down to that most basic level and look hard at how you are setting your people up to succeed. It starts with letting your people know what success looks like in the first place. If you're doing that, now you can provide the tools, the training, the systems, and the processes to meet those standards consistently.

You have to be able to set realistic but lofty standards of performance that move your team and organization toward where you want to go. However, these standards are something that can be attainable

THE CULTURE BLUEPRINT

if you bring the right people into the organization. Standards of performance fill this role in your business, on your team, and within your organization.

JOB DESCRIPTIONS

We've talked about the concept of having standards of performance, so let's get into the practical application of how that should get done. The first thing that you can to do establish qualified standards of performance is to create an effective job description. Basically, someone needs to know what they're getting into. They need to know what they need to do to be successful in the role that they are potentially going to play.

You need to be very clear on what your expectations are. The ambiguous approach that we see in so many job descriptions really serves to set someone up to fail—you know, the famous "other duties as assigned." At most places, that basically means, "Hey, we can throw anything on your plate and you just deal with it."

The reality is, the more specific you are, the better off everyone will be. You can now rest assured that everyone is on the same page from day one. In any good relationship, the clearer your expectations are as early as possible, the better off everyone will be over the long haul. Let's be specific and focus on what is most important.

While there may be other duties as assigned when you go forward, in reality, they probably need to make up 10% or less of what's going on. Instead, what are the most important things for which this prospective employee is going to be responsible? Focus on those.

What are the things that are going to be the biggest drivers in that particular role moving toward the vision

CHAPTER 5: STANDARDS OF PERFORMANCE

you have for the business? You have to establish what those most important things are, because this is how you will be able to measure whether or not they have done a good job. If everyone has a shared and accurate understanding of the expectations and everyone is pulling that proverbial rope in the same direction to meet the standards of performance in all of their respective jobs, then that's how success happens.

To make this start to come to life, I find it helpful to first identify up to four of the most important things that this person is going to do in their job to facilitate the overall success of the organization. All too often, when we read a job description, there may be seven, eight, ten or more duties as assigned. They aren't usually weighted and no one ever explains which of that long list is really most important. However, if you can drill down and focus on what the most critical items are, then that's what you will use in order to be able to judge the success (or lack thereof) of this person and their work.

ASSESSMENT

After you have specified what the job entails, next you need to consider how this person is going to know whether or not they've met the standards of performance. While the assessment piece probably won't go on the job description you post, on a website, or anything like that, it is still an important consideration as you move forward in helping our team members grow.

Your people need to know what standards they need to meet if you are going to achieve your vision. Whatever those three or four most important tasks or responsibilities or roles are and however you have defined them, how can your people succeed in them?

THE CULTURE BLUEPRINT

How do they achieve what they need to achieve to feel like they did great work?

As we've covered previously, most people *want* to be good at what they do. In most settings, it is a rare person who shows up for work and says, "Look, I really want to be below average today." So with that in mind, you need to consider how can best set them up so that they know exactly what success looks like. You should be able to show them in painstaking detail what a successful day looks like in their role.

You can use a number of questions to guide your discussion. For example, what would they be spending their time on? What are they going to be focused on? How will they know, at the end of the day, that they had a good day or that the job was well done? I think we don't do enough of this. We fail to take the time to show our team members what success looks like because we just assume that people are very good at modeling behavior.

Most people are very good at meeting expectations when they're clear. Where leaders tend to get into trouble is when things are left open-ended and we expect people to read our minds or assume that they know what we're thinking. Rarely—if ever—does it work out that way.

Instead, all parties involved would be well served if, as their leader, you either show them what a day in the life should look like or you provide someone else who can. The more specific you are, the better you can figure out if they're a fit for you. At the same time, they can also figure out if *you* are a fit for *them*. This is key, because if someone is happy and excited about their role and they know it—not just the job title, the compensation, or the perks, but the actual day to day practical part of the role—now you've got someone

CHAPTER 5: STANDARDS OF PERFORMANCE

you can work with. Perhaps most exciting, now you've got someone we can help to shape and mold and develop into a great team member.

At the same time, you've got points of accountability that you can use to guide them on their journey along with the big picture items like values and the vision. You have to make sure that they understand that those three or four things that are their most important responsibilities and how they tie to the big picture. They have to understand the values so they know how the organization makes decisions. That has to be made clear to them, as well.

GROWTH

Ultimately, if you want people to think of this as more than just a job and as more than just a paycheck, you have to tell them how they're going to be making an impact. You need to help them see how what they do helps the organization reach that vision and how it impacts the people that you're serving. It is so easy for someone to get caught up in the day to day technical pieces of their job and not think about how the benefits of their work are really impacting others' lives. But when you consider how each team member is adding value to the people who you serve and making the organization better in the process, it makes assessment all the more impactful. And that's when growth begins to not just happen under direction but spread and flourish throughout the team organically.

If you're clear on these aspects of the job, you are purposefully setting your team members up to succeed. But let's keep it real, here: this is not foolproof. This is not something that you're always going to be 100% at on hiring. However, if you want to give yourself the best chance of finding the right fit

THE CULTURE BLUEPRINT

for the roles that you have and setting them up so that they're in a position they can thrive, this is how you do it.

So how do you get them to continue to meet these standards that you've established? The first thing that you have to do is to understand that it can't be a bait-and-switch. You have to either stay congruent with that initial job description, or, if you're going to change the role, then you change the description to match. This needs to be discussed and negotiated. You can't just arbitrarily throw something on someone's plate and expect them to thrive in it. Instead, you need to go back through that same process you went through to create the initial job description in the first place.

You need for them to understand all the things that we just discussed and make sure that they're still a fit. Returning to Jim Collins' *Good To Great* analogy, you can't just switch their seat on the bus without telling them. Everything that you do needs to be congruent—the training, the reinforcement, the way you're evaluating their performance, and the way that you're giving them feedback—it all absolutely has to be consistent with that initial description and that initial role that brought them to your team to begin with.

Along those same lines, you need to recognize them when they do something well. You need to catch people doing things right and you absolutely must

> *You need to catch people doing things right and you absolutely must reinforce the standards you set.*

CHAPTER 5: STANDARDS OF PERFORMANCE

reinforce the standards you set. At the same time, you should always be striving to reinforce the vision and the values. You need to help your team members grow within those borders day after day (we'll explore this further in Chapter 8: Communication). But you need to make sure that this is top of mind.

Deep down, your individual team members probably have a loose understanding of what you're expecting of them, but you want this to be something that they know intimately. You want them to eat and sleep their purpose so that when they are on the job and making decisions, it is a no-brainer: it is just their automatic, nearly reflexive reaction. In order to get to that level of function, you have establish expectations, assess progress, and the foster growth you've all agreed upon. And when you do so, all parties win.

That's how you develop someone.

If someone can really go out there and be an ambassador for your organization, that means you've done a great job reinforcing the standards that you expect and all the things that go into that. Then you need to have some sort of structured performance review. I hesitate to use the word "formal," because formality is not a word I'd use to describe the way that I approach most things. However, you need a structured performance review so that you can help your team members understand where they are doing well, where they could stand to grow, and how they might consider shifting their focus to better align with organizational/team and/or personal goals.

Unfortunately, many times a performance review is just telling someone about the mechanisms to get a raise or to ascend within the organization. Other times, it is simply an opportunity to give somebody an "attaboy" and tell them, "Hey, great work!" But

THE CULTURE BLUEPRINT

all too often, when someone wants a pay raise or we're talking about a promotion or whatever else, the organization lacks a structured way to help someone understand when it might be reasonable to expect those things.

Instead, the assessment piece we've described here helps the team member better understand what they can expect their role to be moving forward and what they can look forward to as a part of the organization. The structured performance review gives them this benchmark. It's a little bit like a report card. It's just an update. It doesn't need to be something that triggers fear or anxiety. However, this structured time lets us communicate to them that we will spend the time to analyze where they are and where they would like to be moving forward.

At the leader, the performance review also affords you the opportunity to have the conversation to discuss how performance has been measured, what the results have been so far, and to respond however is appropriate to trigger further growth. It's a great way to define when you are going to change someone's compensation instead of doing so arbitrarily. If raises are not linked to such specific metrics, goals, or objectives, then an

> *If raises are not linked to such specific metrics, goals, or objectives, then an important opportunity to reinforce desired behavior is squandered.*

CHAPTER 5: STANDARDS OF PERFORMANCE

important opportunity to reinforce desired behavior is squandered.

You're not saying, "Hey, you did this, this, and this really well, and that merits more from our organization, that merits a bigger opportunity. That merits more money." But if we can link it to the things that we established as our objectives in the beginning, now we've set this precedent that they understand. They are likely to see the connection and think, "If I meet this sort of standard of performance, then it's going to help me ascend toward my best possible career within the confines of this organization."

WORK IT OUT

Write down at least 3-5 standards of performance that you would say are critical markers of success in your current role?

How would you measure or quantify each of the standards you wrote above in order to determine your effectiveness in meeting those standards?

6 Systems

CHAPTER 6: SYSTEMS

WHY SYSTEMS?

Systems are processes through which our people are empowered to succeed in meeting our standards of performance. It doesn't matter if we're talking about a client in a training facility or a coach on a sports team; your systems are simply the standard steps toward success that your team or our organization take as part of your culture.

But what do these systems look like? Most simply, if your team or organization has encountered some level of success, it probably begins by documenting what you do well. You are basically saying "Hey, we want to do things this way every time because we're creating a standardized way to meet our standard of performance." What is more, you should have standards in everything you do—t doesn't matter what role someone plays within your organization.

It doesn't matter if it is a client, a team member, a coach, or a player; everyone has a standard that they have to meet if the team or organization is going to achieve the vision. For example, if it is a training client, in order for you to achieve your vision of the impact you want to have on clients' lives. The client has to hold up their end of the bargain, too. The way they go about their business when they come in for a training session matters. You have to give them

THE CULTURE BLUEPRINT

a system that they can follow that is thorough and complete, potentially all the way from how they enter the facility to how they warm up and including how they complete their training session.

In sports, athletes have to do this constantly. As a coach, I was always considering how we prepared for practice, how we started practice, and how we transitioned to certain segments during practice. There should be a consistent way of doing things that becomes "our" way of handling your business. Everyone within the organization should be able to recognize and take ownership of the idea that, "This is the way we do things to achieve our goals to play at a championship level."

That's the idea, at least. You want to be able to consistently meet your organization's standards of performance, and then you can have confidence that if you have given a team member your system and you have groomed them and taught the system well, then they should be able to effectively execute it. Some of this is a question of aptitude, but your systems can make this process as seamless as possible.

Many self-proclaimed experts would tell you that systems aren't just for supporting your efforts but rather one of the most important things in all your business. I think this dates back to when franchise operations manuals were massive 500+ -page books. People would brag about how exhaustive and comprehensive their systems were. However, at their core, systems need not be this overwhelming, daunting thing. Instead, they are just documenting what you do well so that you can do it well all the time. It need not be any more complicated than that.

If you think about it, we do this all the time as coaches. Basically, a training program is a system

CHAPTER 6: SYSTEMS

of how we want someone to come and spend their time in the gym. When you're developing your system, keeping this comparison in mind can be particularly helpful. Most undamentally, systems are a documented, repeatable way of doing things well that have already proven effective.

What you do not want here is theory. You do not want untested processes because you have no way of knowing whether they will lead to the desired outcomes (standards of performance) you are trying to achieve. Simply put, systems are a mechanism to set your people up to succeed on a consistent basis.

In the next chapter, we will dive deeper to discuss how you can actually create or document your systems in a practical and concise manner that will make the idea of systems come to life so that you can not only create but implement your systems. Even more importantly, you'll find that it will be far easier for your people to be able to abide by these systems consistently in order to help the organization and the individuals achieve the larger culture goals.

BUILDING OUT YOUR SYSTEMS

Once you recognize the value of systems and how they can positively impact your culture and your team, you need to consider how to actually construct them in order to give your people the best opportunity to succeed. Once you have considered the role that systems play in the bigger picture of building your ideal culture and the way that they fit in, you are ready to begin. But as has long been said, *starting is the hardest part.*

Once you get over your fear of systems themselves, next, most people usually have to overcome the fear of actually building them. Mentally,

THE CULTURE BLUEPRINT

many people make system construction into a daunting, overwhelming, and intimidating task when in reality, it doesn't have to be. It is so much more simplistic than we usually choose to make it.

Understand that over time, I've done all sorts of things that really built up this whole concept of creating systems. When I was a college baseball coach, I had a playbook that was 136 pages long and it detailed every facet of our program. It described approaches to everything that we were going to teach from pitching, to outfield play, to base running, and beyond. It discussed and described pretty much everything that we did.

This was great because it got all the members of the team to a common understanding. It was common language. Fast forward several years down the road and I built two franchise operations manuals. These documents were used collectively with 265+ franchisees, and just like before with my baseball team, it was a lot of information to the point of being overwhelming. For me personally, any time someone mentions how they need to document and create their systems, I picture them holding those massive operations manuals or big playbooks. But the truth of the matter is that all we should be doing is documenting what already works.

If something is already working, there's often more demand for us than we personally have the ability to supply. For example, in sports we were talking about documenting the plays that we want to run or the situational strategy we planned to use. I documented the offensive approach I wanted my team members to take. When viewed through that lens, then our systems are nothing more than documenting what we want to accomplish and the way we want

CHAPTER 6: SYSTEMS

to accomplish it so that someone else can execute it. Nothing more. Nothing less.

It's no more complicated than that, but that doesn't mean we don't try to make it that way. We think that we have to write everything down, and it's this really detailed page after page series of checklists. But that's not how most people learn.

If I were to say, "Okay, I want you to map out a training program for a distance coaching client," one of the things that you would likely do would be to share videos of how exercises are to be performed because that's the easiest way for you to teach those things to someone from a distance. If they can't watch you demonstrate them in person over and over, then video is our next best option. That's the simplest way that we can craft most of our systems. Most of our systems can be developed by simply videoing the offline tasks that we perform.

It doesn't matter if we're talking about how to field a ground ball in baseball or if we're talking about how to do a movement screen with a client: if we can video it, it is going to be so much easier for someone to learn. In some circles, it isn't just the best alternative to in-person—it may even be the best option *period*.

Don't believe me? Consider this:

I coach my son Alex's youth baseball team. It's a team for players age seven and under. One of our players had played other sports but had decided he wanted to give baseball a shot. While most of the kids on the team already had a couple years of playing under their belt, this particular young man was going to have to work to catch up.

Recently during a game, he slid into third base and did this perfect hook slide. I mean, we're talking about something so pretty that I couldn't get my

THE CULTURE BLUEPRINT

college players to do it so well when I was coaching college baseball.

At any rate, he laid down a perfect hook slide.

The other coach on our team looked at him and asked, "How did you learn to slide like that?"

Without hesitation, the young player replied right back, "I watched YouTube videos."

> *"I watched YouTube videos."*

There are fewer and fewer readers these days. Sadly for me because I'm definitely somebody who gravitates to reading and writing a lot, most people today are more interested in consuming information in video format. Particularly younger people tend to be more visually-driven than ever. If you can document these processes that you do in video format, they'll follow them. They can review them. They'll learn them.

That's it. That's how people learn to replicate a behavior. They learn a skill by investigating how to do it online. Their preferred method of skill acquisition is to go to YouTube and watch a video then try it out. It is quick, easy, free, and can be viewed over and over again. So why aren't we just documenting what we do in that video format?

If you want to get your people to really execute what you're asking them to do, you need to create systems so that they can meet the standards of performance. Practically speaking, the first thing that you need to do is think about is your format. And to me, video is the easiest thing.

This can take multiple forms. For offline or asynchronous tasks, you can use a smartphone. If you can mic someone up or use better lighting to make

CHAPTER 6: SYSTEMS

sure that the production quality is enhanced, then that's even better. But worst case scenario, as long as you can see and hear what the presenter is doing and saying, it can be a powerful teaching tool.

If it's an online or synchronous approach, then you can use screen capture software like Camtasia or Jing and capture it that way. In this circumstance, you narrate what you are doing as you are doing it, demonstrating exactly what you expect along the way. As a result, you have provided clear expectations of your standards of performance that can be revisited by the team member whenever they wish, making it effective, efficient, and lasting. All you are really doing is documenting them so that someone else can basically follow your footsteps, and using video allows that to happen almost organically without hundreds of pages or weeks of time spent.

PUTTING YOUR SYSTEMS INTO ACTION

As effective as the previously-described approach can be, not every task lends itself well to the strategy of simply recording a video. In these cases, how do you make this a systematic blueprint for someone to execute everything they need to execute in order to be successful? First, return to the job description. Consider the tasks that go on in your organization that each person has to complete in order to successfully meet his or her standards of performance.

What tasks have to be accomplished on a regular basis, whether they be daily, weekly, or monthly? List them. Odds are, you're going to come up with on the order of 20-30 things that have to be done. We then further define those tasks, deciding whether they are offline or online tasks then we just have someone follow us and we go through that task. You

THE CULTURE BLUEPRINT

demonstrate it so that someone else can model your behavior.

Once that is complete, you can now upload this document into a private membership area of your website or set the YouTube videos to private and share the links. If you want to go even further, perhaps you could provide the same information via a mobile app that is even easier to access. And as the example, I know that either I can do it exactly the way that it needs to be done or I can provide an example of someone who can so that I can clearly convey the expected standard of performance. It's the simplest thing.

I don't understand why people are so hesitant to embrace this, because it makes the whole concept of creating systems so much more accessible. It is the simplest thing that you can do to ensure your long-term success. The beautiful thing about this is that if you were just putting together a checklist of how to perform a particular task, you'd most likely miss something. Someone would have to interpret what you wrote and you're hoping that you're writing it in a way that they're going to understand so that they perform it the same way that you did.

It's almost impossible to do that (this is coming from someone who writes on a daily basis). It's almost impossible to adequately describe complex skills in words without some level of miscommunication. However, if you provide a video and your team members can see you actually what you are talking about, then you are concisely demonstrating it in the exact way you want it done.

Whether it be the facial expressions that you have, the posture that you use, the timing or the rhythm of what you're accomplishing, everything can be detailed

CHAPTER 6: SYSTEMS

down so that if there is something important to communicate, it is being captured. All the nuances can be shown, so now modeling that behavior becomes so much easier. It is the easiest way for them to learn and it is the easiest way for you to set them up for success.

Be sure to put this into action very quickly, because the quicker you do this, the easier it is going to be for your people to succeed. It doesn't matter if we're talking about an athlete on the field, or an employee in your business—if they can see it and they can apply it, you're going to get immediate results.

At the same time, having it easily accessible so that it can be revisited is key, too. Providing a resource that can be consulted wherever and whenever is light years superior than the tired approach where you think, "Oh, we're going to train something in a staff meeting once a month." The ability to consume the information and then learn to apply it and revisit it whenever is so much simpler in this format.

CREATING SYSTEMS BUY-IN

Having created two successful franchises, I can tell you that people would frequently come in and say, "Well, I just want systems." They think that it's this magical thing that's going to be the bridge from this chaotic environment where everything seems disjointed and ineffective to this smooth-running, perfectly oiled organizational mechanism. In truth, that's not really what a system is.

All a system does is to produce a documented and repeatable way of how we've done something right. The next person can do the same thing and meet a standard of performance that moves them toward their goals simply by following the system. However, as hungry as management seems to be for systems, the

THE CULTURE BLUEPRINT

team members who are "in the trenches" sometimes need a little coaching in order to understand their power.

The first thing we need to do is educate them as to why the system exists in the first place. Why is this activity important? Why is this process necessary? How does it tie to the bigger picture? Because if you want true buy-in, you need to help people understand why they're doing things. At the same time, once they see the value in the system, then the culture you've fostered can dictate that perhaps they will find a way to improve it once they understand the bigger picture.

As such, it's your job to make them understand why your organization or team has done it this way. Once they understand why you have done it this way and what you're trying to achieve, their experience may lead them to be able to refine it for enhanced effectiveness. They may see your system and think to themselves, "Well, you know what? We could do it a little bit better this way." We see this frequently with people when we encourage them to focus on the process more than the outcome. An example of focusing on the outcome might be memorizing a checklist of steps. On the other hand, focusing on the process might involve considering the possible areas of improvement and opportunities for enhanced efficiency.

With a team member, you're teaching them new skills. You are teaching them new behaviors that ultimately can serve to move the organization leaps forward. But your systems cannot be so rigid that they can't adapt and change over time as they are implemented. The best cultures encourage constant refinement and reinforcement of the systems. They should never be "one and done."

CHAPTER 6: SYSTEMS

As the leader, you can't just say, "Hey, go watch these videos. Come back here and know how to do things our way." If you want people to do things your way, then you need to be invested on an at least a weekly basis. But, in some cases, with small teaching moments, this could even occur on a daily basis.

It can be as simple as giving someone two or three minutes of feedback after you see them out on the floor doing something. Just saying, "Hey, you know what? I noticed you did this. You did this great. There was one thing that I'd like to see us try to reinforce, one thing that maybe we could tighten up for next time." Providing guidance and reinforcement for behaviors you want to see more of and suggestions for improving or eliminating things you want to see less of is a great strategy for growth.

This approach alone can serve to reinforce that your team members are an extension of you. They are ambassadors of your organization and you've been able to scale up, thereby allowing you to have more impact. You've been able to go out and do more great work, because it's no longer all on your shoulders.

THE PROCESS

Most fundamentally, systems can be boiled down to a five step process: tell, show, do, review, reinforce. It's a simple approach that I've seen time and time again work. And consistently, I've seen and enjoyed far superior results using this concise strategy than alternatives consisting of inches-thick, mind-numbing operations manuals.

Tell your team the expectations, both verbally and in writing. Show your team exactly what you expect with as much clarity and detail as possible, remembering just how powerful video can be

THE CULTURE BLUEPRINT

as a tool here. Allow your team members to try it out themselves in a relatively safe, low-stakes environment. Mentor and coach them up with a debrief session immediately after they do for the first time. Reinforce what you saw and heard that you liked and provide suggestions for growth and change for the things you didn't.

It's not just the way that we document knowledge. It's the way that people learn. Use this powerful approach in implementing any and all of the systems that you want to leverage to further success.

CHAPTER 7: PEOPLE

WORK IT OUT

How would you define business systems and what role do you see them playing in your business success?

What is the five-step process to business systems implementation? How do you see it working in your unique business situation?

THE CULTURE BLUEPRINT

 *People*

CHAPTER 7: PEOPLE

MORE THAN PEOPLE

If you are not setting your people up to succeed, then they are not going to thrive. When you first opened this book, you may have been surprised that a culture book didn't even mention people until the seventh chapter. Most people think that great culture begins with the organization's people. You're likely to hear it over and over: "Hey, if you've got great people, you'll have great culture." But I am quick to tell you: that is not necessarily the case.

I've seen organizations from sports teams to Fortune 500 businesses undergo a sudden change in leadership and suddenly go from highly successful to dysfunctional seemingly overnight. That might be the only difference—the change in leadership. The organization might have team members in place who are thriving. Then the next thing you know they are struggling and there's mass attrition.

So what happened?

These people didn't go from being great people to bad people. But they didn't connect with the new leadership, either. They didn't connect with the vision. They didn't connect with whatever the new set of values might be. While everyone seems to think that if you bring in great people then you're bound to have a great culture, the truth is, if you are not setting

THE CULTURE BLUEPRINT

your people up to succeed, then they are not going to thrive—no matter how good they might be.

It's no different than a sports team where an athlete gets into the right situation and they thrive. They go from a role player or even a disgruntled distraction to someone who is consistently contributing. They are scoring more points. Their batting average is higher. They are pitching more effectively. Everything suddenly lines up for them.

On the other hand, when they were on the wrong team, they struggled. The situation change didn't make them a better or worse person. It didn't suddenly make them a more talented or less talented player, either. But, put in the right situation or put in the right organization with the right leadership, they suddenly began to reach their potential. They're going to be doing more than just showing up and punching the clock.

CONNECTING WITH THE VISION

As the leader and the curator of the culture, you have to make sure that you are bringing people onto the team who connect with your vision. That's what we see when we think about the people component of building a great culture—you have to set your people up to succeed. But where should that begin?

First, anyone who is new to the team absolutely must connect with the vision that you have, with who you are, with what your organization is about, and where you are trying to go. If a potential new addition to the team is motivated and inspired by the plans you have already made, then they are probably going to be more likely to push themselves to do more. They are more likely to be actualized.

Actualization is the process by which people

CHAPTER 7: PEOPLE

reach their fullest potential. It is difficult for an individual to be actualized through internal means and motives alone. We all need to feel like our skills, knowledge, values, and other tangibles and intangibles are contributing to the bigger picture, and the organization's vision are a critical part of that equation.

> *Actualization is the process by which people reach their fullest potential.*

OPERATING THROUGH THE VALUES

While our vision is the first point of connection, if your people buy into your organization's values, then they will be empowered to make successful decisions. If individual and organizational values are similar, then the way your people make decisions is not going to be so different than the way the organization needs to make decisions to be successful. However, if a team member's value structure is completely different and doesn't line up with those of the organization, then it may be difficult to get them to fully commit to the larger effort.

We know the damage that regular turnover can create. There is plenty of research and information out there regarding the cost of turnover within an organization. In some industries, the cost to hire and train a new person can run upwards of five figures and for upper management, it isn't uncommon for such change to eclipse six figures. However, if we have continuity and consistency with the makeup of our team, then things get smoother. Time and money are saved. We can conserve energy to focus accomplishing goals rather than staffing our team.

Our people simply have to connect with the vision and the values.

COMMUNICATING THE STANDARDS OF PERFORMANCE

The values and the vision can be communicated as part of the recruitment phase and may be considered more "big picture" forms of expectation. However, the closer an applicant or potential team member comes to actually joining the team, the more important it may be for them to consider the specific expectations conveyed in the standards of performance.

All too often, we bring in people because it is convenient or because they have an impressive resume. We shouldn't get overly enamored with a resume alone, when you consider the fact that any resume worth the paper it was printed was designed to be the most positive reflection of the person submitting it. Even if is 100% accurate, it only means that person was able to meet someone else's standards of performance adequately. You need to consider if you are prepared to put your people in the best position to meet your organization's standards of performance regardless of how remarkable their application materials may be.

USING THE SYSTEMS

Are your people—whether new or long-term members—willing to consistently follow the systems you have in place? I frequently talk to entrepreneurs in the personal training industry who hire trainers

CHAPTER 7: PEOPLE

with significant experience. It isn't uncommon to hear them speak of hiring fitness professionals with a decade or even two of experience working with clients in various gyms and as personal trainers.

I'll frequently say, "Well, this person may have a great resume and plenty of experience, but if they don't line up with your vision and don't intend to operate within your values, then they're probably not a good fit." If they're used to doing things their own way, they are not likely to follow your system. That will likely make it challenging for them to meet your standards of performance.

This is a far better issue to consider before hiring rather than after. An applicant may be a great person or even a talented fitness professional, but they just may not be a great fit. Hiring great people is not—by itself—the answer. However, hiring the right people who are the right fit and setting them up to succeed is how we build a great culture.

On the other hand, if you are not setting them up to succeed, they may still be a great person, but they're going to be a short-timer with your organization. They will be off looking for a different opportunity where they are inspired by the vision and where the values align with their own personal values. They will be looking for opportunities where the standards of performance are things that are clearer to them and that they feel confident that they can meet them. If we do not have those things in place, your organization will be little more than a job rather than a career.

ADDING TO YOUR TEAM

We've recognized the role that people play, and yes—they're the heart and soul of having a great culture—but they are not the entirety of having a great

THE CULTURE BLUEPRINT

culture. The only reason that you need to bring people in is that the demand for what you offer exceeds what you can personally provide. If this is the case, you need to consider the type of person you intend to hire, what you are asking them to do, and how you are going to empower them to succeed.

It is easy to be blown away by applicants with lots of experience, but the truth is that for many positions, that is probably the wrong approach. If your business is growing to the point that you need more help, then that's evidence that your systems are working reasonably well. That's not to say that you couldn't stand to improve even more with the right hire, but in most cases you aren't trying to add capabilities to your team as much as you are looking to add capacity. You have limited bandwidth and if business is good, that can become a bottleneck. What you need most is the ability to do more of what you are already doing. As such, you don't need someone to come in and completely retool things.

In most cases, the more important variables that we're looking for are things like people skills, work ethic, and an ability to be punctual. You want any hire to be passionate about the field, passionate about service, and to align as closely as possible with your vision and values while meeting your standards of performance and following your systems.

Whoever this new hire ends up being, you need this individual to have the attitude and the aptitude to succeed within your organization. If this person meets all those criteria and they've got some experience, now you've got the makings of an incredible person to bring on to your team. But you need them to meet those criteria first.

On the other hand, if they happen to be really

CHAPTER 7: PEOPLE

strong but they pull in the wrong direction, it can be to the detriment of your organization. It can almost be like a cancer within the team. You absolutely must find people who align with what you are trying to do. These people can be ambassadors for what you're trying to accomplish and add to the overall capacity of your team in the process.

> *If you look at great companies, they're usually represented by great people on the front lines.*

If you look at great companies, they're usually represented by great people on the front lines. The best teams have surgical precision when it comes to placing the right personalities right out front where they can represent their organization in the most visible and proper way.

For example, when I think about the people at Disney, or the people at Starbucks, or the people at the Apple store, they're usually pretty much in line with the organization as a whole. They are passionate about the things their companies provide and that passion is readily apparent. The people at the Apple store are so excited about Apple products and the technology they have. The people at Disney embody that "Disney persona" and contribute to the company's vision of creating "the happiest place on Earth." The only way Disney, Starbucks, or Apple are going to get those people is to have this vetting process and these standards upfront.

If you go to the Apple store, they're probably not trying to hire someone who has 30 years of tech

THE CULTURE BLUEPRINT

experience as their number one priority. Instead, they are looking to hire someone who meets their other criteria and they will provide training and education for the technical aspects of the job. Likewise, Disney is the same way. They're hiring those smiling faces for the front lines. They've got certain traits and characteristics—sometimes referred to as "soft skills"—more than they've got an extensive arsenal of technical knowledge or "hard skills."

There are plenty of things that we can do in the interview process to make sure. We can ask people to jump through hoops and make them qualify themselves time and time again. I've been in situations where I would ask people to send in a video. Other times I would give someone specific directions on an application. This weeds out a lot of people because if they are not that committed to this opportunity, they will not follow through.

I've also been in a situation where I would require resumes to be hand delivered to me. That way, I would get a quick first opportunity to see what type of first impression an applicant might be able to make. If they aren't able to do it there when they are supposed to be on their best behavior, then we probably don't need to spend any more time pursuing them. When I'm looking at bringing someone into our culture, the fit is critical and strategies like this can be a big benefit.

It's a lot like the old adage you hear in real estate, "You make your money when you buy." You need strategies to help you find that person out of the gate who fits so that they can help lift everyone else up. This is how you can get the right people onboard these strategies can help you filter through some noise to quickly determine who is going to complement our existing team the best.

CHAPTER 7: PEOPLE

What To Look For: Aptitude

While this aspect of any person can vary substantially depending on the position we are trying to fill, you are still most basically looking to see if a potential hire has the knowledge, skills, and abilities necessary to be successful in the role. You need to be clear that you are not asking them to come in and transplant whatever they did in their previous job or their previous career here because, frankly, if that was where they wanted to be, they'd be doing it there still.

A number of questions can help you determine an applicant's readiness for your position. Do they have good people skills? Are they going to be prompt? Are they going to reflective of the way that you want to connect with people? How is their work ethic?

I understand that these are subjective things but that's why you go through the interview process. It doesn't necessarily matter if they already have experience in all those things. What does matter is whether or not they're capable because you are going to be asking them to do things your way anyway.

What To Look For: Attitude

While aptitude speaks to experience, ability, or knowledge, attitude speaks to the more subjective "want to" factor. Do they have the personality to want to be successful in this role? Do they get the vision that your organization has? Are they excited about it? Do their personal values at least line up pretty well with your organizational values? Are they excited about those three or four big action items that they're going to be responsible for and do they embrace the things that are the drivers of your business?

Asking and answering this question can help you decide whether or not an applicant has the

THE CULTURE BLUEPRINT

appropriate personality to be capable of succeeding in this role.

What To Look For: Fit

Lastly and certainly related to aptitude and attitude, you need to assess whether or not an applicant fits in with the culture that you have worked so hard to establish. Are they someone who is going to connect with your clientele? Are they someone who will fit in well with the existing team members? Perhaps most telling: are they someone who you could see yourself enjoying spending time with and you feel like you would enjoy mentoring?

If that is not who they are, it is going to be very difficult for you to do a great job as a leader if there's not a connection. When I think about hiring somebody, I ask myself bluntly: "Do I like this person as a person?" It seems so simple. Do I like this person as a person? Because if I don't, we're probably not going to be great at giving them the skills that they need. You probably are not going to be great at developing their aptitude and giving them the competency that they need to grow.

Ultimately, if it's not a fit, it is okay to move on. There's a reason why people say, "Hire slow, fire fast." It is because so often people hire in situations of urgency. They lost an employee and they are understaffed. They are scrambling. "I have got to find somebody."

Instead of saying tapping the brakes and checking to see who is a good fit, who has the potential to thrive in the role that we have, and who might be best suited personally to the role we have need for on our team, we rush to solve the problem so that we can get back to all the other problems we have to solve. But a bad hire

CHAPTER 7: PEOPLE

can create far more problems than it solves. We owe it to ourselves and our team members to do our best to get it right.

But how?

Internship Programs

So, fine. You get it. You understand that it may be the philosophical or "soft skills" that are more important than a mountain of experience in helping your organization grow. But how do you find these people and how do you bring them onboard?

When you look at some of the most successful organizations in your field, chances are they have some form of formal internship program. For example, in the fitness industry, leaders like Boyle Strength and Conditioning or Cressey Sports Performance have extensive, established, and highly competitive internship programs. They're always developing people.

What's great about this is that it can serve as a vetting process where you get to catch someone early in their career and they get to experience what you do. The people who really embrace your vision, values, standards of performance, and systems can then be fast-tracked for part-time or even full-time opportunities in your organization in the future.

It's a little like in the professional baseball ranks. It's a little like having a farm system. You are teaching people your way and you are seeing who would be a good fit to perform at this level long-term. At the same time, they are getting to feel things out on their side, accruing valuable practical experience in order to be able to answer the question as to whether or not your organization is somewhere they could see themselves working more long-term.

THE CULTURE BLUEPRINT

Personal Referrals

While an internship program can be a great way to grow your team from within, it probably shouldn't be your only source for talent. If you either haven't built an internship program or perhaps it hasn't produced an appropriate candidate for an opening you have, you'll obviously have to look externally. So where should you look?

The first place I think you should look is within your personal network. I always begin by looking to the people who I already know. I ask people I trust and with whom I already have a relationship. If that still doesn't produce the results you are after, you can look to a second tier of people that they know who perhaps you do not. Ideally, if you can know them or at least get a referral, then you are going to have a much better chance of everything lining up, giving you a higher probability of success.

Don't limit yourself here, either. Be creative and innovative. Maybe it is someone who has been active inside your business in another role, even as a client or customer. Alternatively, maybe it is someone who you know from different social or civic circles you are both a part of. Even if it happens to be an indirect or secondary relationship, mutual connections can be a great source because they probably understand whether a potential relationship might be a good fit or not.

Beyond that, then and only then will I begin to go completely to the cold-call route and look outside my sphere of contact. However, those places are where I would prefer to start. And, frankly, I would say that 80% of the hires that I've made in the last 10 years have come from warm leads.

CHAPTER 7: PEOPLE

Advertised Searches

Once you've exhausted those preferred channels of hiring and still haven't identified a suitable candidate, how do you still hold these criteria in place with more traditional routes to hiring? You can certainly advertise through normal channels or via more modern channels like social media.

You could run ads through trade associations or certifying bodies. You could market any number of ways that you want. What's more important than *where* you market is *what* you're marketing. You have to be clear about what the expectations are and about the type of person that you want.

It's almost like creating a sales page. "This is the right person for this job who meets these criteria. The right person for this job would be expected to do A, B and C." That way if someone is going to apply, they know exactly what they are getting themselves into. They have been provided with clear expectations and a concise but complete connection point with your vision and values. It doesn't matter whether you are using a Facebook ad or a placement with a certification body as long as you are making it clear about who you are looking for and what criteria you need them to meet.

SETTING CLEAR EXPECTATIONS

Once you have brought a new team member on board, how do you keep them engaged and empower them to succeed? First, it goes back to establishing clear expectations. You need to think back to those standards of performance that we talked about earlier. Your team members have to know what success looks like. They have to know how they can get there and

THE CULTURE BLUEPRINT

precisely what is expected of them. They need to know whether or not they are going to win or lose. They need to know what it takes to win and what they have to do to thrive. Perhaps just as importantly, if they are failing to meet expectations, they need to know what they have to do differently to get there and to enjoy success.

Beyond that, they also need to know what to do once they have achieved those expectations. What's next? Do they get a raise for that? Do they qualify themselves for other opportunities? Many leaders wonder when they should give raises and how they should be tied to performance and other expectations. It gets much clearer if there are published standards of performance. If a team member is failing to meet expectations, it is fairly easy to justify that they probably shouldn't be compensated more. On the other hand, if they are consistently exceeding them, then it is worth discussing and exploring other opportunities. But first, these standards have to be in place.

Secondly, you need to not only have systems in place, but you need to coach your team members to execute those systems. One of the things that is a bit of a pet peeve of mine in the fitness industry is that although we should be the most well-equipped people in the entire professional world at helping someone thrive and succeed after they join out team, many times we simply don't. Just because we should doesn't mean we actually do, but because what we do for a living is help someone become a better version of themselves—someone who is better equipped to achieve their goals—one might think that this comes natually. Unfortunately, such is not often the case.

We bring on someone new to our team and say, "Here's your employee handbook. We're going to

CHAPTER 7: PEOPLE

have a staff meeting once a month," and we just dump things on them. Then we say, "Well we're paying them, so they'll figure it out. It's not our problem anymore, we're paying them so we solved this problem."

In truth, you should be coaching them with the same intensity that you're coaching your clients or your athletes. You should be helping them reach their potential. You should be approaching it in the same way that you figure out what success looks like to your customers with specific standards of performance. But much of the time, for whatever reason, we just don't.

Instead, you need to figure out where they are today and what you need to do to bridge that gap. That's the program you need to designing for them and your systems are going to be part of that program—just like exercises are going to be part of a training program.

You've got to coach them to execute everything.

You've got to coach people to maximize their potential and to meet and exceed those standards of performance in order to fulfill their potential in the role they can play in your organization. Fitness professionals should be better equipped than anyone else in the world to do this. That's how we help people succeed. Instead, we tend to shoot our wounded and eat our young.

It's time to change that reality. You simply must communicate with them regularly. Treat them like the critical pieces of your business puzzle that they are. Much of this starts with the vetting and recruiting process. You must hire the right people. Bringing the right people into the organization is much like recruiting in college sports. You see high-profile programs sign four and five-star recruits every year who then have trouble leading that roster to success

THE CULTURE BLUEPRINT

on the field or on the court. That's a sure-fire sign of a cultural issue in the organization.

Not long ago, I was consulting with Dallas Baptist University's baseball program. One of the things that I feel like they do far better than most programs in college baseball is player development. They consistently sign a roster full of fairly pedestrian, unheralded, under-the-radar recruits. But they take those same players and the next thing you know they are making the post-season, advancing to super regionals, hosting a regional, and getting numerous players drafted who were very lightly recruited out of high school.

Instead of chasing after high-profile prospects and trying to recruit toe-to-toe with major conference schools, the coaching staff has focused instead on finding the right people to fit their culture. They scour their primary geographic areas looking not so much for the *best* players but the *right* players who buy in to their system, live up to their standards, and compliment the team members who have already connected in a similar way.

That's how they have approached success. It starts in that recruiting process. You're not just looking at measurables like, "Hey, can this kid throw 92? Is this kid tall and lanky and has a good frame?" In the fitness business world, it's no different. "Hey, does this person have a CSCS or are they FMS certified? Do they have ten years of experience?"

You are no longer just staging a who-has-the-most-impressive-resume contest. Instead, you're looking at the aptitude and the attitude that can make them most effective at filling the role you need them to fill. If you can provide the leadership, it is then merely a question of whether or not you have the standards,

CHAPTER 7: PEOPLE

the systems, and the communication in place to help them grow.

GROWING INTO SUCCESS

Simply put, success is no more complicated than giving your team members the standards of performance that you expect in their role and holding them accountable to meet them. You can and should provide the systems for them to follow that will empower them to meet those standards and you should also be in regular communication with them on a regular basis to ensure progress, but it doesn't need to be any more complicated than that.

If you do those things and they are a fit for your organization, you have given them the best likelihood of reaching their potential and being that impact player for you. We often make it more complicated than that because we're just trying to plug a hole instead of saying, "Okay. What's best for the organization long-term moving forward?" Or, we aren't clear about their role so we get a good person but we don't set them up to thrive and we don't see them reach their potential. We fail to create an environment where they're excited to be a part of it long-term. However, if you can follow this big-picture culture-building approach, then you eliminate that and give your organization the best chance to have sustainable and meaningful success.

//
8
Communication

CHAPTER 8: COMMUNICATION

COMMUNICATION IS THE LIFEBOAT

We would be remiss if we didn't point out the obvious fact that communication ties everything together. If you have a leader who is able to articulate the vision and reinforce the values consistently, it allows everyone to be on the same page. Clear, concise, and accurate communication unifies. Anyone who is a member of the team or organization would benefit from reinforcement so that they know they are on the right path and moving in the right direction. When you communicate effectively as the leader, you are reinforcing the vision, the values, and the standards of performance that you are meeting that are moving your organization toward realizing them.

When I get called in to consult with a leader or a team with a business that is struggling, many of the problems can be traced back to a breakdown in communication. People aren't clear about what those standards of performance look like. They're not clear about what the vision is. Then, you also have to recognize that anyone who you are working with—regardless of what kind of high-performer they may be—is first and foremost a person. They're not just a machine. They're not just a transaction. They're not just an asset. You have to treat them accordingly.

THE CULTURE BLUEPRINT

You have to demonstrate to them that you value them and you have to communicate that regularly because you need to recognize them for the things they do well. You should reinforce all the framework of your organization repeatedly, as well. You can't just assume that your team will know.

You have to make sure that everyone is clear, because if there is clarity, it is much easier to succeed. If you know what you are trying to accomplish and your team understands that, as well, then it is an easier task to accomplish it. I see this all the time: people think that they can have a 15-minute weekly meeting, or have a huddle every handful of days. Or maybe they have a monthly staff meeting and they think that's enough.

In truth, you need daily communication. You need to make sure that each member of your team is pulling in the same direction. It doesn't have to be high-volume of communication. It's certainly more an issue of quality than quantity, but you need to provide continual reinforcement of what you are trying to do and where you are trying to go.

You also need to recognize people when they do things right. Your organizational culture should encourage your team to catch people doing things right. There are times when it may be necessary to re-evaluate or course correct to get someone back on the right path. Otherwise, if they stray off course without correction, they may drift too far and that's when bigger problems occur. However, if you are consistent and providing feedback daily, then you're more likely to notice when a team member begins to drift off track.

Regular communication also affords you the

CHAPTER 8: COMMUNICATION

opportunity to reinforce your values. This is the essence of the system that you are trying grow and it can serve to keep small problems small before they can turn in to something so much bigger.

BRINGING IT HOME

Hopefully by now you see how these components all fit together and how strong leadership sets the tone for instilling that culture of success. You can see how values really are just simply the guardrails to keep you in line to achieve your vision. You understand how standards of performance are most basically just your job description: here's the role and here's the part you play in us achieving this vision. You can also see how systems are just ways to meet those standards of performance on a consistent basis, and how setting your people up to succeed will make your organization so much more effective in achieving its aims. Lastly, you can also understand that part of the way that you set them up to succeed is by being clear about everything and consistent in your communication.

You have to understand how these pieces fit together, because the whole is far more valuable than the sum of its parts. Culture is not an a la carte buffet but rather a carefully orchestrated symphony that requires each piece playing its role fully in order to be most effective and impactful. You have to have all the pieces in place. You can't just pick and choose and say, "Well, yeah I'll have great people and that will cure everything else." Or, "I'll have great systems and that will mask everything that we have that's a problem."

That's not how it works.

What is really reassuring to me is that you now know what the framework is. You know what the components are, and if you see a problem, you just

THE CULTURE BLUEPRINT

have to clean up whichever piece is deficient, maintain what's good, and grow from there.

Oh yeah—one other thing: culture isn't a destination to which you can arrive. It is a journey. And on the journey, as the leader, you should set the tone and grow yourself. Encourage your team members to grow and provide them with the ideas, the tools, and the resources to improve over time. Because together you can grow stronger than you ever could alone.

Enjoy the journey!

CHAPTER 8: COMMUNICATION

WORK IT OUT

How would you say your typical communication strategies have **helped** you in building a positive culture? What has worked best about what you have been doing?

How would you say your typical communication strategies have **hindered** you in building a positive culture? What has been the biggest challenge in doing what you have been doing?

ABOUT THE AUTHORS

Pat Rigsby
www.patrigsby.com

Pat Rigsby is a dad, husband, business coach, entrepreneur & author. He's built over 30 different businesses, including two Entrepreneur Franchise 500 award winning franchises. Today he coaches entrepreneurs to create their Ideal Business, one that allows them to earn more, have a greater impact, and enjoy more freedom to live the life of their dreams.

Toby Brooks
www.tobyjbrooks.com

Toby Brooks is a dad, husband, professor, author, coach, entrepreneur, and speaker. He is an Associate Professor and Program Director of Athletic Training at the Texas Tech University Health Sciences Center in Lubbock Texas. After completing his PhD at the University of Arizona, he has spent the past 20 years working with athletes and students at all levels across the globe. His mission is to help excellence-driven people from all walks of life relentlessly pursue Better Every Day.

www.ingramcontent.com/pod-product-compliance
Lightning Source LLC
LaVergne TN
LVHW041341080426
835512LV00006B/560